The Making of Urban Europe, 1000–1994

I will tell the story as I go along of small cities no less than of great. Most of those which were great once are small today; and those which in my own lifetime have grown to greatness, were small enough in the old days.

HERODOTUS

FIGURE 6-1

Estimated Numbers of Legal Abortions and Related Government Policy Actions, 1966–1996

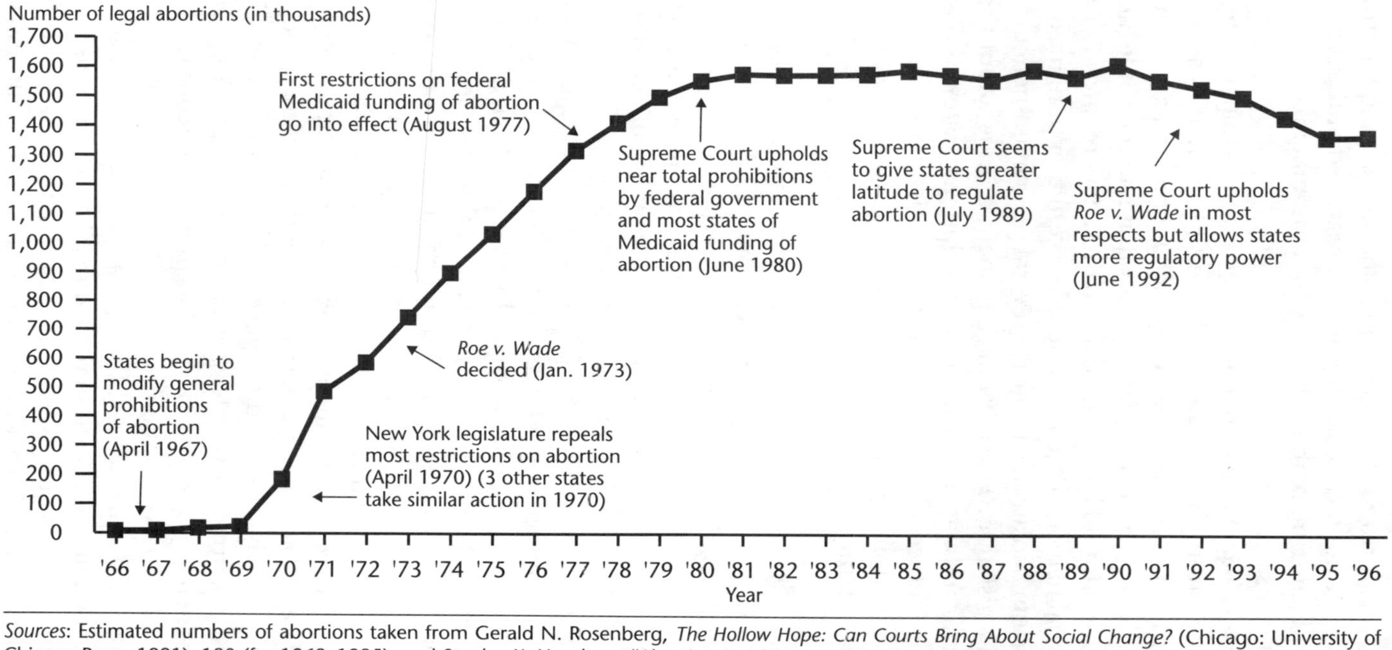

Sources: Estimated numbers of abortions taken from Gerald N. Rosenberg, *The Hollow Hope: Can Courts Bring About Social Change?* (Chicago: University of Chicago Press, 1991), 180 (for 1968–1985); and Stanley K. Henshaw, "Abortion Incidence and Services in the United States, 1995 and 1996," *Family Planning Perspectives* 30 (November–December 1998), 264 (for 1986–1996).

and pressures against providing abortions, ranging from disapproval in the local community to threatened and actual violence. This decline helps to explain the lower numbers of abortions in recent years.

Roe v. Wade has had an unexpected political impact. The decision greatly strengthened the developing movement against legalized abortion by creating a perceived need for action and a target to attack. By the same token, the groups that had sought legalization of abortion found it difficult to maintain their strength after their major goal had been accomplished. As a result, opponents of legalized abortion had an advantage for several years in influencing elections and legislation. This advantage helped to bring about the array of federal and state restrictions on abortion that followed *Roe.* And the Court helped to create a situation in which abortion is a major issue in national politics, one that affects government action on a variety of other issues.

Political Dissent. In its First Amendment cases, the Supreme Court often reviews government policies aimed at people who take unpopular political positions. The Court has a mixed record in these cases, but over the last four decades it has made a number of decisions limiting censorship and punishment of political dissenters. In the 1960s it struck down government policies that penalized people for association with groups on the far left. During the Vietnam War it issued decisions shielding opponents of official U.S. policy from punishment for their activities. In an era without such direct confrontations between government and political dissenters, the Rehnquist Court has established some additional protections. For instance, it struck down criminal penalties for burning the flag as a political statement, and it limited economic retaliation against public employees and business owners who criticize government policy.

The impact of these decisions is difficult to measure, but in all likelihood they have limited government action against dissent and thus encouraged dissenters. For instance, the Court's protection of opponents of the war in Vietnam probably encouraged the open expression of opposition.

Yet the Court has not brought about a massive increase in the level of political dissent in the United States. One reason is that the Court's support for political dissent has not gone as far as it could have. Another is that government officials do not always comply with the letter of the Court's decisions, and non-compliance with their spirit is quite common. But perhaps most important are conditions in the private sector. For one thing, most people simply do not hold and want to express the highly unpopular views about political matters that the Court has sought to protect.

Further, people realize that the Court cannot prevent all the negative consequences of political dissent. People may refrain from saying what they think because they fear that employers will fire them, friends and neighbors will ostracize them, or people in the community will attack them. The black parents who fought against inadequate and segregated schools in the South often had to deal with severe economic pressures and violence. Similarly, threats and violence have been directed against environmentalists who oppose economic activities that are important in their area. Some opponents of government-sponsored religious activities experience property damage, harassment, and death threats.[83] When one father opposed mandatory student drug tests in a rural Texas school, he was fired from his job and faced what a reporter called "life as a pariah."[84] It is not surprising that people often choose to remain silent rather than face such consequences. This result underlines the limits on the Court's ability to change basic social realities.

Racial Equality

In debates over the Supreme Court's impact, no issue is given as much attention as racial equality. The Warren Court of the 1950s and 1960s did a great deal to combat racial discrimination. It ruled against discrimination in education and voting, it upheld federal laws prohibiting discrimination, and it sought to protect the civil rights movement from legal attacks. To a degree, that line of policy extended back to the Court of the 1940s and forward to the Court of the 1970s. Implicitly, the Court was making a commitment to improve the status of black Americans. To what extent have the Court's policies achieved that goal?

Change in Status. The first question to ask is how much the status of black Americans has changed. This is the subject of considerable disagreement, in part because progress has varied so much among areas of life.

Politically, racial barriers to black voting in the South were overcome. This change contributed to growth in the number of black elected officials in the country, from about 300 in 1965 to 9,000 in 1998.[85] And white officials, especially in the South, have become considerably more willing to respond to black concerns.

Socially, the segregation of American life has broken down unevenly. Segregation of hotels and restaurants went from a standard practice to an anomaly. Legally segregated school systems have disappeared from the Deep South and the border states, but the level of actual segregation among schools remains high and has increased somewhat since the 1970s.[86] This school segregation reflects the high level of housing segregation, which has declined little since 1970.[87]

Economically, discrimination in employment has not disappeared, but it has declined considerably. This decline and substantial growth in education levels have helped to bring about a major improvement in economic status, but the disparity between the races remains wide. Indeed, the ratio between the average incomes of blacks and whites has not changed much since 1970, remaining at about 60 percent both for individuals and for families. And black children are more than twice as likely to live in poverty as white children.[88]

The Court's Impact. To the extent that progress toward racial equality has occurred, how much can be ascribed to the Supreme Court? Certainly there are other important sources of change, including the other branches of government, the mass media, and the civil rights movement itself. In some respects these sources are considerably more powerful than the Court.

The Court's relative weakness is clear in education and voting, the areas in which it was most active. The Court's rulings against dual school systems and devices to limit black voting in the South had only limited effects in themselves. It was the enactment of the Civil Rights Act of 1964 and the Voting Rights Act of 1965 and their vigorous enforcement by the Johnson administration that broke down official school segregation and made the right to vote effective.

Because constitutional protections against discrimination do not apply directly to the private sector, the initiative in attacking housing and employment discrimination had to come from the other branches. Congress enacted statutes in the 1960s that mandated equal treatment in these areas, and the executive branch has enforced them. In the 1970s and early 1980s the Court generally gave broad interpretations to the laws against employment discrimination and thus strengthened them. There is evidence that these laws have had a significant impact on the economic status of black citizens, and the Court's decisions might be given a small degree of responsibility for that impact.

Perhaps the Court had important indirect effects, in that its early civil rights decisions helped to spur passage of federal legislation and strengthened the civil rights movement. The development of a mass civil rights movement in the South was probably inevitable, and the Supreme Court was hardly the major force contributing to its development. But the Court may have speeded the movement's growth. Its decisions in education and other areas created hope for change and established rights to be vindicated by political action. This is especially true of the *Brown* decision, which had considerable symbolic importance for some people.[89] The Court's protection of the civil rights movement itself did not eliminate the harassment of civil rights groups in the South or the violence against their members, but the Court helped the movement to withstand the pressures placed on it.

The series of civil rights laws adopted from 1957 on also may owe something to the Court. In education and voting, the Court initiated government action against discrimination and helped to create expectations that Congress and the executive branch were pressed to fulfill. It is true that congressional action was most directly responsible for bringing about school desegregation in the Deep South. But if the Court had not issued the *Brown* decision, Congress might have had less impetus to act against segregation at all.

An Assessment. The issue of racial equality illustrates both the strengths and limitations of government in achieving societal change. Public policy has helped to bring about significant reductions in the disadvantages of black Americans. But these disadvantages have hardly disappeared, and even a stronger government commitment to equality could not have eliminated them altogether.

For the Supreme Court specifically, the assessment is also mixed. The Court has had little direct impact on discrimination in the private sector. Even in the public sector, it has been weak in the enforcement of rights. But it has helped to initiate and support processes of change, and its members probably can take some credit for progress toward racial equality. If the Court's effects have been far more limited than many people had hoped, the Court has contributed to significant social change.

Conclusion: The Court, Public Policy, and Society

It is now possible to reach some general conclusions about the role of the Supreme Court as a public policy maker. As this chapter and Chapter 5 suggest, that role is fundamentally limited in some respects but still quite important.

The most obvious limitation on the Court's role is that it addresses only a small number of issues. In many policy areas, the Court rarely makes decisions. To take the most important example, the Court is a minor participant in the making of foreign policy. And it plays only a small part in many fields of significant judicial activity, such as contract law and family relations.

Even in its areas of specialization, the Court intervenes only in limited ways. It makes decisions on a small sample of the issues that affect the rights of criminal defendants or freedom of expression. And the Court has been cautious about substituting its judgment for that of Congress and the president.

When the Court does intervene, its impact is often reduced by the actions of other institutions and individuals. A ruling that public schools must eliminate organized prayers does not guarantee that those observances will disappear. Efforts to broaden freedom of expression may be stymied by conditions in society that the Court cannot influence.

These limitations must be balanced against the Court's strengths. Certainly a great many Supreme Court decisions have significant direct effects. Antitrust decisions determine whether companies can merge. School desegregation decisions determine the schools that students attend. Interpretations of the Voting Rights Act shape the course of local politics. The effects of capital punishment decisions are literally matters of life and death for some people.

The Court also helps to shape political and social change. Its partial opposition to government regulation of private business was ultimately overcome, but the Court slowed a fundamental change in the role of government. If *Roe v. Wade* was not as consequential as most people think, it *has* been the focus of a major national debate and struggle for more than a quarter century. The Court's decisions have not brought about racial equality, even in conjunction with other forces, but they have helped to spur changes in race relations.

As the examples of abortion and civil rights suggest, the Court is perhaps most important in creating conditions for action by others. Its decisions help to put issues on the national agenda so that other policy makers and the general public consider them.[90] The Court is not highly effective in enforcing rights, but it often legitimates efforts to achieve them and thus provides the impetus for people to take legal and political action. Its decisions affect the positions of interest groups and social movements, strengthening some and weakening others.

The Supreme Court, then, is neither all-powerful nor insignificant. Rather, it is one of many public and private institutions that shape American society in significant ways. That is a more limited role than some have claimed for the Court. But the role that the Court does play is an extraordinary one for a single small body that possesses little tangible power. In this sense, perhaps more than any other, the Supreme Court is a remarkable institution.

NOTES

1. *Engel v. Vitale* (1962); *Abington School District v. Schempp* (1963).
2. U.S. Congress, Senate, *Congressional Record,* daily ed., 103d Cong., 2d session, February 3, 1994, S725.
3. *Lee v. Weisman* (1992).
4. *Santa Fe Independent School District v. Doe* (2000).
5. *Jaffree v. Board of School Commissioners,* 554 F. Supp. 1104, 1128 (S.D. Alab. 1983).
6. Phillip Rawls, "James, Moore Resist Prayer Ruling," *Chattanooga Free Press,* November 5, 1997, A3; George McEvoy, "Alabama Governor's Crusade Includes a Supreme Insult," *Palm Beach Post,* May 11, 1998, 17A. The decision was *Chandler v. James* (M.D. Alab. 1997).
7. *Seif v. Chester Residents Concerned for Quality Living* (1998).
8. *Bragdon v. Abbott,* 524 U.S. 624, 655 (1998).
9. Rex Bossert, "Asbestos Case Deepens Rift in 5th Circuit," *National Law Journal,* February 16, 1998, A6.
10. Linda Greenhouse, "Justices Narrow the Uses of Forfeiture," *New York Times,* June 23, 1998, A14.
11. *Ortiz v. Fibreboard Corp.,* 527 U.S. 815, 831 (1999). The earlier decision was *Amchem Products, Inc. v. Windsor* (1997).
12. "Harassment Case Heard by High Court is Settled," *New York Times,* February 10, 1995, A25.

13. The Court's decisions were *Shaw v. Reno* (1993); *Shaw v. Hunt* (1996); and *Hunt v. Cromartie* (1999, 2000).
14. *Grumet v. Pataki* (N.Y. Ct. App. 1999); Lisa W. Foderaro, "Hasidic Public School Loses Again Before U.S. Supreme Court, But Supporters Persist," *New York Times,* October 13, 1999, B5.
15. See, for instance, Donald R. Songer, Jeffrey A. Segal, and Charles M. Cameron, "The Hierarchy of Justice: Testing a Principal-Agent Model of Supreme Court–Circuit Court Interactions," *American Journal of Political Science* 38 (August 1994): 673–696.
16. R. Shep Melnick, *Between the Lines: Interpreting Welfare Rights* (Washington, D.C.: Brookings Institution, 1994), 253–255.
17. Christopher P. Manfredi, *The Supreme Court and Juvenile Justice* (Lawrence: University Press of Kansas, 1998), chap. 7.
18. See Michael J. Berens, "Punishing the Poor," *Columbus Dispatch,* September 25, 1994, 1A, 2A; and Berens, "'Hook 'Em and Book 'Em,'" *Columbus Dispatch,* November 18, 1996, 2A.
19. Harrell R. Rodgers Jr. and Charles S. Bullock III, *Law and Social Change: Civil Rights Laws and Their Consequences* (New York: McGraw-Hill, 1972), 75.
20. *Green v. School Board* (1968); *Alexander v. Holmes County Board of Education* (1969).
21. *Missouri v. Jenkins* (1990); *Spallone v. United States* (1989). On *Spallone,* see Lisa Belkin, *Show Me a Hero: A Tale of Murder, Suicide, Race, and Redemption* (Boston: Little, Brown, 1999).
22. *United States v. Dickerson* (4th Cir. 1999), *Dickerson v. United States* (2000).
23. Stewart G. Pollock, "The Court and State Constitutional Law," in *The Burger Court: Counter-Revolution or Confirmation?* ed. Bernard Schwartz (New York: Oxford University Press, 1998), 248–250.
24. Richard A. Leo, "The Impact of *Miranda* Revisited," *Journal of Criminal Law and Criminology* 86 (Spring 1996): 652–653. See also Paul G. Cassell and Bret S. Hayman, "Police Interrogation in the 1990s: An Empirical Study of the Effects of *Miranda,*" *UCLA Law Review* 43 (February 1996): 887–892.
25. Leo, "Impact of *Miranda* Revisited," 663. See Stephen J. Schulhofer, "*Miranda*'s Practical Effect: Substantial Benefits and Vanishingly Small Social Costs," *Northwestern University Law Review* 90 (Winter 1996): 507–510, and David Simon, *Homicide: Life on the Killing Streets* (Boston: Houghton Mifflin, 1991), 193–207.
26. *California Attorneys for Criminal Justice v. Butts* (9th Cir. 1999). See Jan Hoffman, "Police Are Skirting Restraints to Get Confessions," *New York Times,* March 29, 1998, 1, 21.
27. *Harris v. New York* (1971).
28. Nat Hentoff, "Will Miranda Make It?" *Washington Post,* January 15, 2000, A25.
29. Jerome H. Skolnick, *Justice Without Trial: Law Enforcement in Democratic Society,* 3d ed. (New York: Macmillan, 1994), 277 (emphasis in original).
30. Bradley C. Canon, "Is the Exclusionary Rule in Failing Health? Some New Data and a Plea against a Precipitous Conclusion," *Kentucky Law Journal* 62 (1974): 702–725; Myron W. Orfield, Jr., "The Exclusionary Rule and Deterrence: An Empirical Study of Chicago Narcotics Officers," *University of Chicago Law Review* 54 (Summer 1987): 1024–1049; and Craig D. Uchida and Timothy S. Bynum, "Search Warrants, Motions to Suppress and 'Lost

Cases': The Effects of the Exclusionary Rule in Seven Jurisdictions," *Journal of Criminal Law and Criminology* 81 (Winter 1991): 1034–1066.

31. Skolnick, *Justice Without Trial,* 279.
32. Thomas Y. Davies, "A Hard Look at What We Know (and Still Need to Learn) about the 'Costs' of the Exclusionary Rule: The NIJ Study and Other Studies of 'Lost' Arrests," *American Bar Foundation Research Journal* (Summer 1983): 611–690.
33. Harold J. Rothwax, *Guilty: The Collapse of Criminal Justice* (New York: Random House, 1996), 41. See L. Timothy Perrin, H. Mitchell Caldwell, and Carol A. Chase, "If It's Broken, Fix It: Moving Beyond the Exclusionary Rule," *Iowa Law Review* 83 (May 1998): 727–732.
34. *United States v. Hollingsworth* (7th Cir. 1994). The Supreme Court decision was *Jacobson v. United States* (1992).
35. Elliot E. Slotnick and Jennifer A. Segal, *Television News and the Supreme Court: All the News That's Fit to Air?* (New York: Cambridge University Press, 1998).
36. *Matsushita Electric Industrial Co., Ltd. v. Epstein,* 516 U.S. 367, 388 (1996). A recent example is *United States v. Montero-Camargo,* 208 F.3d 1122 (9th Cir. 2000).
37. See Anne Freedman, *Patronage: An American Tradition* (Chicago: Nelson-Hall, 1994). The major decision was *Rutan v. Republican Party of Illinois* (1990).
38. Michael J. Berens, "Holding the Purse Strings," *Columbus Dispatch,* November 19, 1996, 1A, 2A.
39. J.W. Peltason, *Fifty-eight Lonely Men: Southern Federal Judges and School Desegregation* (Urbana: University of Illinois Press, 1971), 9.
40. "Parents Stage Demonstration," *New Orleans Times Picayune,* November 24, 1960, quoted in Robert Coles, *Children of Crisis: A Study of Courage and Fear* (Boston: Little, Brown, 1967), 385 n. 2.
41. *Singleton v. Norris,* 108 F.3d 872, 873–874, 876 (8th Cir. 1997).
42. *Khan v. State Oil Co.,* 93 F.3d 1358, 1363 (7th Cir. 1996).
43. Robert Justin Goldstein, *Burning the Flag: The Great 1989–1990 American Flag Desecration Controversy* (Kent, Ohio: Kent State University Press, 1996), 64–66. The decision was *Johnson v. State* (Texas Ct. Crim. App. 1988).
44. William K. Muir Jr., *Prayer in the Public Schools: Law and Attitude Change* (Chicago: University of Chicago Press, 1967); Richard Johnson, *The Dynamics of Compliance* (Evanston, Ill.: Northwestern University Press, 1967).
45. *United States v. Shipp* (1909). See Mark Curriden and Leroy Phillips Jr., *Contempt of Court* (New York: Faber and Faber, 1999).
46. Robert Satter, *Doing Justice: A Trial Judge at Work* (New York: Simon & Schuster, 1990), 227.
47. Marcia Coyle, "Fourth Circuit No Longer a Star Pupil," *National Law Journal,* July 10, 2000, A4.
48. David G. Savage, "Crusading Liberal Judge Keeps High Court Busy," *Los Angeles Times,* March 3, 1996, A3.
49. See Beth Berselli, "Clinton to Sign Credit Union Bill," *Washington Post,* August 5, 1998, D9, D16. The decision was *National Credit Union Administration v. First National Bank and Trust Co.* (1998).
50. William N. Eskridge Jr., "Overriding Supreme Court Statutory Interpretation Decisions," *Yale Law Journal* 101 (November 1991): 338; updating through 1996 is from Lori Hausegger and Lawrence Baum, "Behind the

Scenes: The Supreme Court and Congress in Statutory Interpretation," in *Great Theater: The American Congress in Action,* ed. Herbert F. Weisberg and Samuel C. Patterson (New York: Cambridge University Press, 1998), 224–247.

51. *Federal Baseball Club, Inc. v. National League of Professional Baseball Clubs* (1922).
52. Beth M. Henschen and Edward I. Sidlow, "The Supreme Court and the Congressional Agenda-Setting Process" (Paper presented at the annual meeting of the Midwest Political Science Association, Chicago, April 1988); Michael E. Solimine and James L. Walker, "The Next Word: Congressional Response to Supreme Court Statutory Decisions," *Temple Law Review* 65 (1992): 425–458; Melnick, *Between the Lines,* 261–264.
53. Eskridge, "Overriding Statutory Decisions," 348, 351, 359–367.
54. J. Mitchell Pickerill, "Judicial Review and the Lawmaking Process: The Role of the Supreme Court in the Legislative Process" (Paper presented at the annual meeting of the Midwest Political Science Association, Chicago, April 1998).
55. Public Law 105-277, Sec. 1403 (1998).
56. Louis Fisher, "The Legislative Veto: Invalidated, It Survives," *Law and Contemporary Problems* 56 (Autumn 1993): 273–292. For a different interpretation, see Jessica Korn, *The Power of Separation: American Constitutionalism and the Myth of the Legislative Veto* (Princeton: Princeton University Press, 1996), 39–40.
57. Bruce Fein, "Judge Not," *New York Times,* May 8, 1997, A23. The decision was *United Steelworkers v. Weber* (1979).
58. U.S. Congress, House, *Congressional Record,* 89th Cong., 1st sess., 1965, 111, pt. 4, 5275. See John R. Schmidhauser and Larry L. Berg, *The Supreme Court and Congress: Conflict and Interaction, 1945–1968* (New York: Free Press, 1972), 8–12.
59. William G. Ross, *A Muted Fury: Populists, Progressives, and Labor Unions Confront the Courts, 1890–1937* (Princeton: Princeton University Press, 1994).
60. The decision was *Food and Drug Administration v. Brown & Williamson Tobacco Corp.* (2000).
61. *Chamber of Commerce of the United States v. Reich* (D.C. Cir. 1996).
62. "Statement Announcing the Benchmarking Process in Federal Procurement," *Weekly Compilation of Presidential Documents* 34 (June 29, 1998): 1213–1214. The decision was *Adarand Constructors, Inc. v. Pena* (1995).
63. Samuel Krislov, *The Supreme Court in the Political Process* (New York: Macmillan, 1965), 140.
64. Dirk Johnson, "Chicago Council Tries Anew With Anti-Gang Ordinance," *New York Times,* February 22, 2000, A14. The decision was *City of Chicago v. Morales* (1999).
65. Elizabeth Garrett, "The Law and Economics of 'Informed Voter' Ballot Notations," *Virginia Law Review* 85 (November 1999): 1536–1538.
66. *Cook v. Gralike* (2000).
67. Steven K. Smith and Carol J. DeFrances, *Indigent Defense* (Washington, D.C.: U.S. Department of Justice, Bureau of Justice Statistics, 1996).
68. Richard A. Posner, *The Federal Courts: Challenge and Reform* (Cambridge: Harvard University Press, 1996), 326.
69. On Congress–Court interaction in civil rights, see William N. Eskridge Jr., "Reneging on History? Playing the Court/Congress/President Civil Rights Game," *California Law Review* 79 (May 1991): 613–684.

70. *General Electric Co. v. Gilbert* (1976).
71. *City of Mobile v. Bolden* (1980).
72. Glen A. Halva-Neubauer, "The States after *Roe*: No 'Paper Tigers,'" in *Understanding the New Politics of Abortion,* ed. Malcolm L. Goggin (Newbury Park, Calif.: Sage Publications, 1993), 167–189.
73. The decision was *Bray v. Alexandria Women's Health Clinic* (1993).
74. Hank Harvey, "A Hanging Judge from Ohio," *Toledo Blade,* October 12, 1997, F3.
75. Paul G. Cassell and Richard Fowles, "Handcuffing the Cops? A Thirty-Year Perspective on *Miranda*'s Harmful Effects on Law Enforcement," *Stanford Law Review* 50 (April 1998): 1132.
76. Susan H. Bitensky and Robert A. McCormick, "School Violence and the Court," *National Law Journal,* September 13, 1999, A22. The decision was *United States v. Lopez* (1995).
77. "B.C.," *Columbus Dispatch,* August 11, 1999, 9E.
78. Lauren Bowen, "Do Court Decisions Matter?" in *Contemplating Courts,* ed. Lee Epstein (Washington, D.C.: CQ Press, 1995), 376–389.
79. See Richard A. Brisbin Jr., "The U.S. Supreme Court and the Rationality of Labor Violence: The Impact of the *Mackay Radio* Doctrine and 'Violence' During the Coal Strike of 1989–90" (Paper presented at the annual meeting of the American Political Science Association, San Francisco, August–September 1996).
80. For differing views on the Court's importance, see Gerald N. Rosenberg, *The Hollow Hope: Can Courts Bring About Social Change?* (Chicago: University of Chicago Press, 1991); Bradley C. Canon, "The Supreme Court and Policy Reform: The Hollow Hope Revisited," in *Leveraging the Law: Using the Courts to Achieve Social Change,* ed. David A. Schultz (New York: Peter Lang, 1998), 215–249; and Michael McCann, "How the Supreme Court Matters in American Politics: New Institutionalist Perspectives," in *The Supreme Court in American Politics: New Institutionalist Interpretations,* ed. Howard Gillman and Cornell Clayton (Lawrence: University Press of Kansas, 1999), 63–97.
81. This discussion of abortion is based in part on Rosenberg, *The Hollow Hope,* 175–201; and Matthew E. Wetstein, "The Abortion Rate Paradox: The Impact of National Policy Change on Abortion Rates," *Social Science Quarterly* 76 (September 1995): 607–618.
82. This discussion is based in part on Stanley K. Henshaw, "Abortion Incidence and Services in the United States, 1995–1996," *Family Planning Perspectives* 30 (December 1998): 263–270, 287.
83. Frank S. Ravitch, *School Prayer and Discrimination: The Civil Rights of Religious Minorities and Dissenters* (Boston: Northeastern University Press, 1999).
84. Jim Yardley, "Family in Texas Challenges Mandatory School Drug Test," *New York Times,* April 17, 2000, A1, A16.
85. Gerald David Jaynes and Robin M. Williams Jr., *A Common Destiny: Blacks and American Society* (Washington, D.C.: National Academy Press, 1989), 238; Joint Center for Political and Economic Studies, "Number of Black Elected Officials in the United States, by State and Office, January 1998," accessed at *www.jointctr.org/databank/BEO.htm* on April 21, 2000.
86. Peter Applebome, "Schools See Re-Emergence of 'Separate but Equal'," *New York Times,* April 8, 1997, A8. See also Gary Orfield, Susan E. Eaton, and the Harvard Project on School Desegregation, *Dismantling Desegrega-*

tion: The Quiet Reversal of Brown v. Board of Education (New York: New Press, 1996).

87. See Lance Freeman, "Minority Housing Segregation: A Test of Three Perspectives," *Journal of Urban Affairs* 22 (2000): 15–35; and Margery Austin Turner and Felicity Skidmore, eds., *Mortgage Lending Discrimination: A Review of Existing Evidence* (Washington, D.C.: Urban Institute, 1999).
88. U.S. Bureau of the Census, *Statistical Abstract of the United States, 1999* (Washington, D.C.: Government Printing Office, 1999), 478, 482, 483.
89. Jesse H. Choper, *Judicial Review and the National Political Process* (Chicago: University of Chicago Press, 1980), 93–94; Bradley C. Canon, "The Supreme Court as a Cheerleader in Politico-Moral Disputes," *Journal of Politics* 54 (August 1992): 637–653.
90. Roy B. Flemming, John Bohte, and B. Dan Wood, "One Voice Among Many: The Supreme Court's Influence on Attentiveness to Issues in the United States, 1947–92," *American Journal of Political Science* 41 (October 1997): 1223–1250.

Glossary

Legal Terms Related to the Supreme Court

Affirm. In an appellate court, to reach a decision that agrees with the result reached in the case by the lower court.

Amicus curiae. "Friend of the court." A person, private group or institution, or government agency, not a party to a case, that participates in the case (usually through submission of a brief) at the invitation of the court or on its own initiative.

Appeal. In general, a case brought to a higher court for review. In the Supreme Court, a small number of cases are designated as appeals under federal law; formally, these must be heard by the Court.

Appellant. The party that appeals a lower court decision to a higher court.

Appellee. A party to an appeal who wishes to have the lower court decision upheld and who responds when the case is appealed.

Brief. A document submitted by counsel to a court, setting out the facts of the case and the legal arguments in support of the party represented by the counsel.

Certiorari, writ of. A writ issued by the Supreme Court, at its discretion, to order a lower court to send a case to the Supreme Court for review. Most cases come to the Court as petitions for writs of certiorari.

Civil cases. All legal cases other than criminal cases.

Class action. A lawsuit brought by one person or group on behalf of all persons in similar situations.

Concurring opinion. An opinion by a member of a court that agrees with the result reached by the court in the case but offers its own rationale for the decision.

Dicta. *See* Obiter dictum.

Discretionary jurisdiction. Jurisdiction that a court may accept or reject in particular cases. The Supreme Court has discretionary jurisdiction over most cases that come to it.

Dissenting opinion. An opinion by a member of a court that disagrees with the result reached by the court in the case.

Habeas corpus. "You have the body." A writ issued by a court to inquire whether a person is lawfully imprisoned or detained. The writ demands that the persons holding the prisoner justify the detention or release the prisoner.

Holding. In a majority opinion, the rule of law necessary to decide the case. That rule is binding in future cases.

In forma pauperis. "In the manner of a pauper." In the Supreme Court, cases brought in forma pauperis by indigent persons are exempt from the Court's usual fees and from some formal requirements.

Judicial review. Review of legislation or other governmental action to determine its consistency with the federal or state constitution; includes the power to strike down policies that are inconsistent with a constitutional provision. The Supreme Court reviews government action only under the federal Constitution, not state constitutions.

Jurisdiction. The power of a court to hear a case in question.

Litigants. The parties to a court case.

Majority opinion. An opinion in a case that is subscribed to by a majority of the judges who participated in the decision. Also known as the opinion of the court.

Mandamus. "We command." An order issued by a court that directs a lower court or other authority to perform a particular act.

Mandatory jurisdiction. Jurisdiction that a court must accept. Cases falling under a court's mandatory jurisdiction must be decided officially on their merits, though a court may avoid giving them full consideration.

Modify. In an appellate court, to reach a decision that disagrees in part with the result reached in the case by the lower court.

Moot. A moot case is one that has become hypothetical, so that a court need not decide it.

Obiter dictum. (Also called *dictum* [sing.] or *dicta* [pl.].) A statement in a court opinion that is not necessary to resolve the case before the court. Dicta are not binding in future cases.

Original jurisdiction. Jurisdiction as a trial court.

Per curiam. "By the court." An unsigned opinion of the court, often quite brief.

Petitioner. One who files a petition with a court seeking action or relief, such as a writ of certiorari.

Remand. To send back. When a case is remanded, it is sent back by a higher court to the court from which it came, for further action.

Respondent. The party in opposition to a petitioner or appellant, who answers the claims of that party.

Reverse. In an appellate court, to reach a decision that disagrees with the result reached in the case by the lower court.

Standing. A requirement that the party who files a lawsuit have a legal stake in the outcome.

Stare decisis. "Let the decision stand." The doctrine that principles of law established in earlier judicial decisions should be accepted as authoritative in similar subsequent cases.

Statute. A written law enacted by a legislature.

Stay. To halt or suspend further judicial proceedings. The Supreme Court sometimes issues a stay to suspend action in a lower court while the Supreme Court considers the case.

Vacate. To make void or annul. The Supreme Court sometimes vacates a lower court decision, requiring the lower court to reconsider the case.

Writ. A written court order commanding the designated recipient to perform or not perform acts specified in the order.

Selected Bibliography

The books listed here may be useful to readers who would like to explore further subjects discussed in this book.

Chapter 1 and General

Epstein, Lee, Jeffrey A. Segal, Harold J. Spaeth, and Thomas G. Walker. *The Supreme Court Compendium: Data, Decisions and Developments.* 2d ed. Washington, D.C.: CQ Press, 1996.

Gillman, Howard, and Cornell Clayton, eds. *The Supreme Court in American Politics: New Institutionalist Interpretations.* Lawrence: University Press of Kansas, 1999.

Perry, Barbara A. *The Priestly Tribe: The Supreme Court's Image in the American Mind.* Westport, Conn.: Praeger, 1999.

Semonche, John E. *Keeping the Faith: A Cultural History of the U.S. Supreme Court.* Lanham, Md.: Rowman & Littlefield, 1998.

Slotnick, Elliot E., and Jennifer A. Segal. *Television News and the Supreme Court: All the News That's Fit to Air?* New York: Cambridge University Press, 1998.

Stephenson, Donald Grier Jr. *Campaigns and the Court: The U.S. Supreme Court in Presidential Elections.* New York: Columbia University Press, 1999.

Chapter 2

Abraham, Henry J. *Justices, Presidents, and Senators: A History of the U.S. Supreme Court Appointments from Washington to Clinton.* Rev. ed. Lanham, Md.: Rowman & Littefield, 1999.

Atkinson, David N. *Leaving the Bench: Supreme Court Justices at the End.* Lawrence: University Press of Kansas, 1999.

Maltese, John Anthony. *The Selling of Supreme Court Nominees.* Baltimore: Johns Hopkins University Press, 1995.

Silverstein, Mark. *Judicious Choices: The New Politics of Supreme Court Confirmations.* New York: W. W. Norton, 1994.

Watson, George L., and John A. Stookey. *Shaping America: The Politics of Supreme Court Appointments*. New York: HarperCollins, 1995.

Yalof, David Alistair. *Pursuit of Justices: Presidential Politics and the Selection of Supreme Court Nominees*. Chicago: University of Chicago Press, 1999.

Chapter 3

Cleary, Edward J. *Beyond the Burning Cross: The First Amendment and the Landmark R.A.V. Case*. New York: Random House, 1994.

Garrow, David J. *Liberty and Sexuality: The Right to Privacy and the Making of* Roe v. Wade. New York: Macmillan, 1994.

Hopkins, Ann Branigar. *So Ordered: Making Partner the Hard Way*. Amherst: University of Massachusetts Press, 1996.

Kluger, Richard. *Simple Justice: The History of Brown v. Board of Education and Black America's Search for Equality*. New York: Knopf, 1976.

Lawrence, Susan E. *The Poor in Court: The Legal Services Program and Supreme Court Decision Making*. Princeton: Princeton University Press, 1990.

McGuire, Kevin T. *The Supreme Court Bar: Legal Elites in the Washington Community*. Charlottesville: University Press of Virginia, 1993.

Perry, H. W., Jr. *Deciding to Decide: Agenda Setting in the United States Supreme Court*. Cambridge: Harvard University Press, 1991.

Salokar, Rebecca Mae. *The Solicitor General: The Politics of Law*. Philadelphia: Temple University Press, 1992.

Sorauf, Frank J. *The Wall of Separation: The Constitutional Politics of Church and State*. Princeton: Princeton University Press, 1976.

Urofsky, Melvin. *Affirmative Action on Trial: Sex Discrimination in* Johnson v. Santa Clara. Lawrence: University Press of Kansas, 1997.

Walker, Samuel. *In Defense of American Liberties: A History of the ACLU*. 2d ed. Carbondale: Southern Illinois University Press.

Wasby, Stephen L. *Race Relations Litigation in an Age of Complexity*. Charlottesville: University Press of Virginia, 1995.

Chapter 4

Brenner, Saul, and Harold J. Spaeth. *Stare Indecisis: The Alteration of Precedent on the Supreme Court, 1946–1992*. New York: Cambridge University Press, 1995.

Clayton, Cornell W., and Howard Gillman, eds. *Supreme Court Decision-Making: New Institutionalist Approaches*. Chicago: University of Chicago Press, 1999.

Cooper, Phillip J. *Battles on the Bench: Conflict Inside the Supreme Court.* Lawrence: University Press of Kansas, 1995.

Epstein, Lee, and Jack Knight. *The Choices Justices Make.* Washington, D.C.: CQ Press, 1998.

Epstein, Lee, and Joseph F. Kobylka. *The Supreme Court and Legal Change: Abortion and the Death Penalty.* Chapel Hill: University of North Carolina Press, 1992.

Maltzman, Forrest, James F. Spriggs II, and Paul J. Wahlbeck. *Crafting Law on the Supreme Court: The Collegial Game.* New York: Cambridge University Press, 2000.

Murphy, Walter F. *Elements of Judicial Strategy.* Chicago: University of Chicago Press, 1964.

Schwartz, Bernard. *Decision: How the Supreme Court Decides Cases.* New York: Oxford University Press, 1996.

Segal, Jeffrey A., and Harold J. Spaeth. *The Supreme Court and the Attitudinal Model.* New York: Cambridge University Press, 1993.

Smolla, Rodney A., ed. *A Year in the Life of the Supreme Court.* Durham: Duke University Press, 1995.

Spaeth, Harold J., and Jeffrey A. Segal. *Majority Rule or Minority Will: Adherence to Precedent on the U.S. Supreme Court.* New York: Cambridge University Press, 1999.

Chapter 5

Epp, Charles R. *The Rights Revolution: Lawyers, Activists, and Supreme Courts in Comparative Perspective.* Chicago: University of Chicago Press, 1998.

Leuchtenburg, William E. *The Supreme Court Reborn: The Constitutional Revolution in the Age of Roosevelt.* New York: Oxford University Press, 1995.

McCloskey, Robert G., rev. by Sanford Levinson. *The American Supreme Court.* 2d ed. Chicago: University of Chicago Press, 1994.

Pacelle, Richard L., Jr. *The Transformation of the Supreme Court's Agenda from the New Deal to the Reagan Administration.* Boulder: Westview Press, 1991.

Rabban, David M. *Free Speech in Its Forgotten Years.* New York: Cambridge University Press, 1997.

Schwartz, Bernard, ed. *The Burger Court: Counter-Revolution or Confirmation?* New York: Oxford University Press, 1998.

Scigliano, Robert. *The Supreme Court and the Presidency.* New York: Free Press, 1971.

Shapiro, Martin. *The Supreme Court and Administrative Agencies.* New York: Free Press, 1968.

Wolfe, Christopher. *Judicial Activism: Bulwark of Freedom or Precarious Security?* Rev. ed. Lanham, Md.: Rowman & Littlefield, 1997.

Chapter 6

Canon, Bradley C., and Charles A. Johnson. *Judicial Policies: Implementation and Impact.* 2d ed. Washington, D.C.: CQ Press, 1999.

Goldstein, Robert Justin. *Burning the Flag: The Great 1989–1990 American Flag Desecration Controversy.* Kent, Ohio: Kent State University Press, 1996.

Keynes, Edward, with Randall K. Miller. *The Court vs. Congress: Prayer, Busing, and Abortion.* Durham: Duke University Press, 1989.

Leo, Richard A., and George C. Thomas III, eds. *The Miranda Debate: Law, Justice, and Policing.* Boston: Northeastern University Press, 1998.

Peltason, J. W. *Fifty-Eight Lonely Men: Southern Federal Judges and School Desegregation.* 2d ed. Urbana: University of Illinois Press, 1971.

Ravitch, Frank S. *School Prayer and Discrimination: The Civil Rights of Religious Minorities and Dissenters.* Boston: Northeastern University Press, 1999.

Rosenberg, Gerald N. *The Hollow Hope: Can Courts Bring About Social Change?* Chicago: University of Chicago Press, 1991.

Ross, William G. *A Muted Fury: Populists, Progressives, and Labor Unions Confront the Courts, 1890–1937.* Princeton: Princeton University Press, 1994.

Sources on the Web

There are many sources on the Supreme Court on the World Wide Web. Some of the most useful sources are listed here. As is true of websites in general, the content of these sites can change over time, and some may disappear altogether.

Supreme Court of the United States at *www.supremecourtus.gov/*. This is the Court's official website. Much of the information on it is intended for visitors to the Court and people who want general information about the Court. The site also includes the Court's rules and the calendar for oral arguments in the current term. One useful feature is a list of lawyers and amici curiae participating in cases in the current term (go to "opinions" and then "counsel listings"). There are links to related government websites.

FindLaw at *www.findlaw.com/casecode/supreme.html/*. This website includes a database of Supreme Court decisions since 1893. Under "Supreme Court resources" it has links to a wide range of other sites, including some of those on this list and several news sources such as newspapers and television networks. Some of the links provide biographical information on the justices.

Legal Information Institute at *supct.law.comell.edu/supct/*. The law school at Cornell University maintains this website. Its primary feature is a database of all Supreme Court decisions since 1890 and important decisions prior to that time. Also included are several other kinds of information on the Court. One useful feature is a list of the cases to be heard by the Court in the current term with a summary of the legal questions to be addressed. Connected with the website is a free e-mail subscription service that sends copies of the syllabi summarizing the Court's decisions on the same day they are handed down. These syllabi are linked to the text of the opinions in each case.

The Oyez Project at *oyez.nwu.edu/*. Professor Jerry Goldman of Northwestern University has created this site, which offers, among other things, an extensive collection of audiotapes of oral arguments in the Court. Another feature is a "virtual tour" of the Supreme Court building.

On the Docket at *www.medill.nwu.edu/docket/*. This site is maintained by the Medill School of Journalism at Northwestern University. It provides news on the Court and extensive information on cases decided in the Court's current term and the preceding term and on cases accepted by the Court and awaiting decision.

Office of the Solicitor General at *www.usdoj.gov/osg/*. This website provides several types of information on the solicitor general's office and on the Court. Especially valuable is a file of briefs filed by the solicitor general's office in the Supreme Court. Another useful feature is the "help/glossary" file, located in "briefs," which defines terms related to the Court and provides information on the Court's procedures. The site also provides considerable information on the solicitor general's office itself, including an extensive bibliography.

The Constitution of the United States of America: Analysis and Interpretation at *www.access.gpo.gov/congress/senate/constitution/toc.html*. For many years the Congressional Reference Service of the Library of Congress has published a massive volume summarizing the Supreme Court's interpretations of each provision of the Constitution, along with citations of the relevant cases. Also included are lists of all federal, state, and local statutes that the Court has declared unconstitutional and all Supreme Court decisions overruled by subsequent decisions. The most recent edition of this volume and the most recent supplement are available at this site.

Case Index

Index